Contents

Introduction

Dear Ladies and Gentlemen, this book "Introduction to Psychodynamic Psychology" is created specifically with the idea to introduce readers into the basic concepts and views of psychodynamic theories in psychology. The book does not claim either comprehensiveness or thoroughness, but I dare to say that it is a nice and useful reading for every lover of the psychodynamic trends in psychology. The book gives a general overview of the ideas and views of the classical psychoanalysis created by Sigmund Freud, the ideas and views of analytical psychology created by Carl Gustav Jung, the ideas and views of the individual psychology created by Alfred Adler and the ideas and views of Neo-Freudianism in the face of Erich Fromm and Karen

Horney. My attempt was to make a light, short, and pleasant for a reading book that would provide every reader with something interesting and accessible from this wide and vast field of scientific knowledge. The book explains and presents many of the main concepts and phenomena in the field of psychodynamics, examining some basic theories about the construction, functioning and typology of the personality from the point of view of the deep life of man, his biographical past and his latent/hidden motives. I wish you pleasant and fruitful minutes with this book. Thank you for your attention and your interest. Best regards, Valentin Boyadzhiev!

About the author

Valentin Boyadzhiev is a trained nutritionist, graduated Master of Psychology in "Psychology and Psychopathology of Development". He has acquired Professional Qualification "Teacher of Psychology" and Postgraduate Professional Qualification "Psychological Counseling in Psychosomatic and Social Adaptation Disorders". He has obtained a Psychoanalysis Diploma and he has specialized in Psychoanalytic Psychotherapy. He is a member of the Association "Bulgarian Psychoanalytic Space", "International Society of Applied Psychoanalysis" and „International Alliance of Holistic Therapists". He is a lecturer on issues related to nutrition, diet, supplementation, food and sports. He is also a teacher and a lecturer in the field of psychology, logic, ethics, law, and philosophy. He has been a school psychologist since 2017. He has been participating annually in scientific conferences on psychology, psychotherapy, dietetics and medicine. His main interest and practice are in the field of psychoanalysis and clinical psychology.

Classic psychoanalysis. Ideas and Views of Sigmund Freud.

Approved or denied, Sigmund Freud influences the culture with his theoretical formulations. He creates a system of ideas, views, notions, concepts and therapeutic techniques, which is called psychoanalysis or soul analysis. In his psychoanalytic theory, he emphasizes childhood sexuality and unconscious motivations in the formation, construction and development of the personality. Freud overcomes Descartes's understanding that the psyche consists only of consciousness and proves that most of the psyche is unconscious, and consciousness is part of the psyche. The presence of an unconscious psyche is part of human nature and has attendance in our lives. According to Freud, Polish scientist Nicolaus Copernicus shows that Earth is not the centre of the universe, and Charles Darwin shows that our ancestors are still staying on the trees and smile at us, they did not come from Adam's rib and they are part of the living creatures. Freud, in turn, shows that in their own behaviour and thoughts people are guided by motives that are unconscious and they replace this unconscious with reasonable "contraption". He says we are not what we think we are. According to psychoanalytic theory, in our lives, there are conscious and unconscious processes. The unconscious ones dominate and have a very important impact on our psychic life. From this point of view, nothing is causeless and accidental. Freud claims that random gestures, mistakes, and dreams are not meaningless at all, but are manifestations of our unconscious thoughts and desires. These unconscious processes of everyday life can be the way to reach the contents of the unconscious, to recognize and understand it. But this process is not easy at all. In the broad sense of the word, psychoanalysis is a doctrine and science of the unconscious psyche. Of great importance to him is the repressed unconscious - the content that was in the consciousness, then it was pushed, suppressed, repressed and non-admitted to consciousness, and can not be realized without help. Therefore, in the therapeutic sense of the word, psychoanalysis is an intervention in the unconscious psyche in order to realize the unconscious, and if that happens the symptoms of the disease go away.

What is to realize/become conscious of the unconscious?
Which side of the realization/awareness heals?

Awareness of the unconscious heals when a person experiences again not the past images, but the feelings because when he experiences the traumatic event once again, his negative significance diminishes or disappears. On the other hand, the suppressed experiences turn into a symptom.

Neurotic persons fantasized three repetitive, switching themes:
1.Secret observation of a sexual act;
2.Rape (physical, moral, sexual);
3.Castration
The problem is which are the source and the themes of fantasizing. To answer this question, Freud turns to the genesis of

human society, to the metamorphoses of the drive at the primitive horde level. Thanks to this he succeeds to decree that there is traumatic inherited unconscious.

According to Freud, there are three forms of the unconscious:
1.Preconscious - what we do not realize, but we can recall (hidden, latent);
2.Repressed unconscious - what has passed into the unconscious, but without help cannot be realized;
3.Phylogenetic (archaic) unconscious - deepest and it is part of the structure of the drive.

A cornerstone not only of psychoanalytic theory but also of cultural and resonance in the other spheres of life and science is the doctrine of drives. In this area, Sigmund Freud has undergone the most profound development. The term "drive" in psychoanalysis is deeply integrated with the term "energy". The special feature in Freud is the consideration of drive/instinct as a carrier of energy, and this is called "drive". The energized instinct is called a drive. The Freudian drive has a source - organic agitation in tissues that accumulates energy. He views the drive as an integration of the bodily (somatic) and psychic. Also, the drive has the goal of bringing energy into inner equilibrium, releasing energy in the context through an object or fantasm, which is experienced as a pleasure. The drive has an object to which it is directed and also possesses a tendency to repeatability. According to Sigmund Freud, psychic life is determined by the drives that are innate and they create a certain inner excitement in us on a biological way. This excitement prompts us to act to reduce it by satisfying our desire.

**Need => Excitement=> Action =>
Satisfaction => Attenuation**

After 1920, Sigmund Freud came to the idea that human functioning had a motive. This motive he sees in the face of the two main tendencies/drives: The first is the so-called **"Life Drive"**. It is characterized by the fact that it creates, preserves and proceeds life. It is a constructive and creative drive. Freud calls him "Eros". The sexual drive has a status that is not discussed in fullness. There is no doubt that it is related to the experience of pleasure. The experience of pleasure gives meaning to life. He discovers that the problem is that the sexual drive is most strongly controlled. Here we have to mention that the realization of the pleasure in social inequality creates chaos. Freud thinks that in the flow of our lives, sexual instinct or the so-called "Life Drive" is stronger and blocks at a significant level the pressure of the aggressive drive, the "Death Drive". He believes that the sexual drive suppresses the destructive tendencies and we must put hope on it. People have an affection to life and partly controls their aggressive drive. According to him, one has an attachment to life and partly controls his own aggressive drive. Freud discovers the fact that the sexual instinct suffers deformities not for biological reasons but for cultural and historical situations. It is true that this instinct maintains the type of homo sapiens. In the sexual act, which is one of the drive's realizations, two tendencies, two impulses, two needs, two inclinations meet. On one side is the sexuality that has a biological origin, and on the other is the socio-cultural directions, that is the model of the realization of sexuality, the choice of partner, etc. There are cultural norms that are needed, but there are ones that deform sexual drive. Freud thinks that the problem of pleasure is that there is more to one, and to others less, and concludes that human life is flowing into the conflict between the drive and the culture and the culture is initially hostile to the drive and does not always allow it to happen within what we call human love. Here we can notice a meeting of two tendencies, a meeting of the cultural and the biological. The impulse, the desire, the urge to realize the sexual act is natural, but the way of realization is cultural. The problem is that there is no harmony in the meeting of the two tendencies.

The second is the so-called "Death Drive".
It is characterized by its destruction, aggression and mortification. He has a necrophilic tendency. This is where the

many disagreements with Sigmund Freud's theory begin. As a witness of the First World War, Freud asks himself "What is the cause of this destruction?". These illogical, destructive phenomena in life make him allow such a basic inclination, namely, "Death Drive". He thinks that mankind cannot overcome its destructive attraction. Freud is a representative of the solid Jewish thought, which means that he is a dialectician. He says that the contradictory in the face of opposites is the fundamental property of being. Every thing has its opposite. There is creation, but there is also destruction. Life is a backward movement to death. He is also a representative of Ernst Haeckel's old German physicochemical school, which says that individual development of man is an abbreviated repetition of the phylogenetic development of humanity. He declares the drives as the main content of human motivation, he calls them "intrusive motives" or an internal terrorist. You can not reverse them, forbid or avoid them. Freud says that by virtue of this conflict, in this functioning is involved the Ego, that is, the face of our consciousness. Here we have to mention that the interpretation of the majority of the sexual drive as absolutized at Freud is quite naive and even "tavern", and the inclination to death of which he speaks creates the "bad image of man".

"Life is a Movement to Death" - Sigmund Freud

The specificity of psychosexual development

Sigmund Freud distinguishes 5 stages of development:
1. Oral
2. Anal

3. Phallic

4. Latent

5. Genital

1. **Oral stages** - from birth to 18 months of age

During this time the baby is completely dependent on the people who take care of it. This dependence defines the only way to satisfy needs and desires, with pleasures mostly oral. There is also the so-called **oral-sadistic stage**. When entering this stage, the child is most likely to start biting.

2. **Anal stage** - from 18 months to 3 years of age.

A time when children learn to meet their parents' requirements, to be clean, to retain certain personal hygiene (the path to the toilet). According to Sigmund

Freud, self-control and self-regulation begin here.

3. **Phallic stage** - from 3 to 6 years of age.

The child's attention is focused on the discovery of gender. This is the period in which we notice gender differences based on learning our own body and comparing ourselves with peers and adults. Children are interested in questions that are related to sexual organs, birth and sexual relations between adults. For this stage is also the clash with one major problem related to solving a significant psychic conflict. Sigmund Freud designates it as **"Oedipus complex"** for boys and **"Electra complex"** for girls. They describe in a symbolic way the unconscious desire of the child to possess the parent of the opposite sex and to eliminate that parent from the same sex. Before the two complexes, there is a so-called **"Sexual castration"** - the understanding of belonging to one sex.

4. **Latent stage** - from the age of 6-7 until the beginning of puberty.

Child interests are not aimed at sexuality. It has been displaced in the background, which, according to Sigmund Freud, is due to the physiological changes in the body and the appearance of the "Super-ego"

5. **Genital stage** - entering sexual maturity – puberty.

Psychoanalytic theory of personality. Structural Theory of Personality.

Strictly speaking, this is the first personality theory created by Sigmund Freud in the twenties of the 20th century. On this theory and its possibilities are written thousands of pages of admiration and criticism, but as one says "despite the harsh criticism already 100 so and more years it does not leave the scene of psychological science because it deals with issues which have a stunning burden for our lives, for the reason that this theory has social, moral, ethical, anthropological resonance on the understanding of human nature". There is no psychological theory that is not based on a certain point of view for a human. Usually, there is a meeting of biological and cultural-historical approaches, and from here unfinished discussions and controversies begin. In Freud's concept of personality, there is something unique about the fact that this theory is built on the dialectics of conscious and unconscious psyche. Dialectics is a science of the fact that the phenomena are contradictory. When something new appears, it contains something old. Such an understanding and view where the presence of the unconscious psychic in the person's psyche shocks humanity. Shocking is that Sigmund Freud creates another image of man. He says, "You are not really what you think that you are", "You are not masters in your own home". He thinks that human behaviour is guided by motifs we do not realize, but in their place, we put reasonable explanations. Freud was the first to characterize the psyche as a battlefield between the irreconcilable forces of instinct/drive and reason, nature and culture, the biological and social. Until the 20s of the 20th Century, he affirms the view that man is the bearer of a conscious and unconscious psyche. After 1920, he is taking a step forward and building a psyche structure. This structure allows the theory to be called "psychoanalytic" or "depth" or "confrontational". In a sense, it is "motivational," and the common name of this theory and the theories that resemble it is "psychoanalytic". The term "dynamic" replaces the term "change". This term describes the change of structures and the interaction between them. According to psychoanalysis, the life of a person is accompanied by an inner conflict that is based on unconscious, primary, sexual, and aggressive tendencies.

What is personality?

According to Sigmund Freud, the personality is a psychodynamic structure of processes in a state of conflict which regulates behaviour. Freud creates the idea of the three structural psychic instances (Id, Ego and Super-ego).

Psychoanalysis is a doctrine of the interaction between conscious, unconscious, and superconscious.

After 1920, Freud made a step forward by structuring the psyche and personality in three instances (structures) - Id, Ego and Super-ego. In these three psychic instances, he sees the unity of the personality. This unity allows a person to be internally roentgenographied. These structures are in a dynamic relationship and are often in a state of conflict.
"Id" - "Ego" – "Super-ego"

But what is hiding behind them?

Id is the unconscious part of the psyche or the psychic apparatus, this part appears before the consciousness, it exists from birth itself. It is the lower layer of the psyche. Id contains everything inherited and repressed which is unconscious. This psychic instance/structure is not a reflection of the outside world, its core is the instinct or more specifically - the drive. Id does not know the outside world and does not know time. He also thinks that people are born with primary instincts/drives and that there is a hierarchy of these instincts/drives. He also raises the hypothesis that the main tendency of the unconscious is satisfaction, which in turn is accompanied by a pleasant experience, and exactly because of that there is no morality, since experiencing pleasure is a natural pursuit and cannot be condemned. Morality could be found in the manner in which we get satisfaction and this manner is designed by the culture. Its goals are immediate fulfilment of desires and pleasure-seeking. In "Id" reigns the "pleasure principle". The psychic energy at the beginning of life is contained in "Id," and later under the influence of the environment, and the accumulation of experience is shared between the "Ego" and the "Super-ego".

"Id" is a carrier of energy and performs functions:

1. Energy function- activates man, presses the conscious (cathexis);

2. Motivational function - it is the cause of our behaviour (obsessional motif/compulsion);

3. Symptom-making function - especially strong symptoms of disrupted incest connections (parent-child);

4. Creative function - when the wishes of Id are blocked, energy can be sublimated into a socially meaningful activity.

Somewhere higher and later the consciousness appears. This part of the psyche Freud marks by the name **"Ego"**. In his view, consciousness evolvingly arises as a structure and process. According to Sigmund Freud, the early development of the "Ego" is related to the attitude the child has towards his or her own body. Through the body it is easy to satisfy the desires of "Id", to "serve" the unconscious, to search for objects to satisfy the drives/needs. The ego knows the outside world. Consciousness works on the "principle of reality," that is, one knows the outside world, the time, the space, and only in the state of consciousness, one can distinguish the real from the fantasy object. "Ego" acquires a role and a value when it becomes clear that it is capable of internalizing/perceiving cultural rules and norms, exercising control and resistance against catharsis/drives/instinct's pressure, to work as something more called "Super-ego"). The ego, the healthy ego, balances things between the instances and the outside world, where Id is a representative of the drive, and the Super-ego is a representative of the culture. "Ego" must take into consideration the wishes of "Id" and "Super-ego".

"Ego" is a conscious instance and its functions are:
1. Interaction of the individual with the surrounding, aiming to provide knowledge about the surrounding.
2. Information and control of the body and the drives.
3. Performing cognitive processes.

The **Super-ego**, in its content, is not a biological structure. This instance occurs between 3 and 5 years of age and develops to the point where it becomes self-control and follows us all our lives. It is content acquired from culture, first through the parents, then through the school and the requirements of the institutions. Sigmund Freud, calls this structure conscience or censorship. In the Super-ego sleeps what we have acquired from parents, teachers, society as a whole. This is the part of the psyche that understands and accepts the rules and norms of culture. Freud says that this is the conscience or censorship, that is the "thing" with which we are controlling ourselves to conform to the others. **What does "Super-ego" do?** It guides (which behaviour is appropriate and which is not), forbids, allows, controls, and all of this is in the form of our consent. It also denies the changes in the environment, that is, what actually happens. If we manifest behaviour incompatible with the Super-ego, we experience a sense of guilt, but if we do not accept certain requirements, we do not feel guilty. **What lies behind the guilt?** The answer is clear - the fear of being rejected by others. When there are fantasmic ideas in the Super-ego that eliminate the value of the other, the justice, and when a morality that overlooks others is respected, this Super-ego acts as a pathology. It is not difficult sometimes to find a person with a hypertrophic Super-ego. The Hypertrophic Super-ego always reduces the value of the Ego and can crush it and depersonalize it. The Super-ego functions as a socially unconscious. "Super-ego" represents our consciousness and moral values, that is, our conscience combined with the desire for ourselves - the "Ideal for ourselves." The "super-ego" helps the "ego" to hold/control the "Id" in his constant quest for satisfying the drives while limiting the liberty of "ego" to enjoy the fulfilment of these desires.

The three structures **Id** - **Ego** - **Super-ego** have a complex internal dynamics, and according to Sigmund Freud, the early years of human life (up to the age of 5-7) and the events that occurred during these years are crucial to the development and formation of the personality. During these years there may be different clashes, traumas and failures in development. Freud believes in the so-called biographical/event factor. It is the idea that the character is formed depending on what happened to the individual. If at a certain stage the instinct/drive doesn't receive satisfaction, the individual will be afraid to go to a higher stage, and thus a fixation is obtained at that stage, and if he receives a flawless and endless satisfaction, he will not want to move further and he will have a fixation on the stage of the satisfaction. If there is a fixation, then at later stages of development, the individual will want this satisfaction that he had at the earlier stage. If an individual is fixated in the oral stage but is already an adult, he can seek satisfaction in drinking, eating and smoking. Such a late fixation accompanied by a return to that passed, but satisfying stage is called regression. Regression is an individual's striving to live in a way that is experienced at an earlier stage. Regression occurs when there is a lot of stress in the later stages. The peculiarities arose out of the early stages appeared in the later stages of personality development.

Stages of development as a tool for the typology of personality:

Oral personality - Here the main area of excitement is the mouth. Middle-aged people who are fixated at this stage have an orality that occurs in eating, smoking, kissing. There is harmony between sexual and aggressive tendencies. They are primarily interested in themselves. They are a narcissistic type of persons. Other people acquire meaning for them through what they give. Oral persons are receiving types of people. They are "cultural beggars". They possess disguised aggression. They are demanding, jealous, impatient, vindictive, pessimistic, suppressed, "if they suck, they won't let go".

Anal Personality - Here the satisfaction of needs and drive is related to the anal appeal. Learning to go to the toilet is a socio-psychic process and it reflects the authority of the parent and the way this authority is used. The middle-aged person who is fixated at this stage is a very cold, peculiar type. He is relieving himself from all the inconveniences, from everything bad. When he does it, he is satisfied, not shamed. He is rigid, firm, impermeable. He possesses a sense of power and control over others. He has a strong interest in how he looks and how he behaves. The main fear of this type of personality is the "fear of losing control." He enjoys the pleasure of acquiring a property. The anxiety of this type of personality is between the two forms of evolutionary reactions "to fight" and "to obey". The transition from oral to anal personality develops from the "give me" position to "do what I say". It can be assumed that this personality is an illustration of the contradiction - release from the inside and demands from the outside.

Phallic personality - This stage is characterized and centred on sexual and aggressive feelings associated with sexual organs and erogenous zones. It is assumed that there is a bit of identification with the Oedipus complex. Fixation here is different for men and women. The man rejects the possibility of castration ("I am great in the eyes of others"). At this stage, the woman identifies herself with her mother. The woman is hysterical (romanticizes life and relationship with the man). Castration anxiety pushes the sexual desire towards the mother and enhances the hatred to the father. The Super-ego, in turn, is the heir of the Oedipus complex and blocks / inhibits the movement towards incest and aggression. Rediscovery of childhood and fixation in later ages is a natural content of the psychoanalytic method. The fixations are related to serious work with the Ego and the Super-ego.

Sigmund Freud's psychoanalytic metapsychology. Taboo and the repressive functions of culture.

"Metapsychology is called the psychoanalytic theory of the unconscious; according to it, each psychic process must be described simultaneously from three points of view - economic (like energy transformation), dynamic (as an opposition of psychic forces) and topographical (as unconscious, preconscious or conscious)."

Taboo and the repressive functions of culture.

The word taboo has two opposite meanings. On the one hand, the word means "sacred," "sanctified," and on the other, it has meanings such as "terrible," "dangerous," "forbidden," "impure." Right here we can find the ambivalence of this word and suppose the ambivalence of the emotional impulses that arise exactly through the taboo. The taboo is expressed in various prohibitions and restrictions. These interdictions are different from religious or moral. These taboo prohibitions are not reasoned in any way; we do not know their origin, they are as though implied for those who obey them. According to Wilhelm Wundt, the taboo precedes all deities and religions and is the oldest unwritten law/ code of humanity. From here is presumed the repressive function of culture. Culture is understood as everything created by man. Also, the cult ("cult"-ure) also suggests a certain dose of sacredness. Culture is a mixture of profanity and sacredness, where the cult cannot be directed only to the material.

In a broad sense, it can be distinguished different types of taboos:
1. Natural / Direct - it is defined and is the result of mana (mysterious force) that weighs on man or object

2. Retransmitted / Indirect - it also derives from the mana but has been acquired or transferred by a shaman, chief or another intermediary

3. An intermediate variant of the first two types - when both factors are present

The taboo may have different purposes:

1. Protection of important persons, objects and others from possible misfortunes.

2. Protection and defence of the weak from the powerful mysterious power "Mana."

3. Protection against the dangers of contact with dead people and corpses, the consumption of certain dishes and others.

4. Ensure the smooth implementation of important life events.

5. Protection of people from gods and demons.

6. Protection of unborn and young children from their particular suggestive dependence on their parents.

Except for these taboo features, we can add that there are permanent and temporary taboos:

1. Permanent taboos are the important persons (shaman, kings, chiefs), the dead, as well as all everything that belonged to them.

2. Temporary taboos are associated with certain conditions such as menstruation, postpartum period, the status of warriors before and after an expedition, with activities such as hunting, fishing and others.

Taboo - these are a number of limitations to the primitive peoples. They do not understand why and they have never asked the question "Why?". But they are convinced that non-observance and violation of any of these rules/laws will be definitely strictly punished. These bans are most often related to some pleasures, freedom of movement and communication. At the root of all prohibitions lies a "theory" that "proves" the necessity of these bans, because of certain persons and places is inherent a dangerous power, transmitted by contact and spreading like some kind of infection. Of course, the intensity of this force is also taken into account because it is not evenly distributed between persons and places.

The strange thing is that we can notice that the one who broke a taboo has become a taboo himself.
That one exactly has become a taboo because he carries in himself the dangerous ability to tempt others with his example. He provokes envy because he is allowed what is forbidden to others.

And in this sense, he is indeed "infected," because he is infected by his example, inciting to imitation, and therefore he must be avoided. It is interesting to note that the taboo refers to everything that is the bearer or source of this mystical feature, but it also denotes the prohibition itself, which derives from this feature. For Wundt, the taboo includes "all customs in which manifest the fear of certain objects associated with cult ideas or actions relating to these objects." According to Wundt, "there is no nation or cultural stage that have escaped the damage caused by the taboo." With the appearance of the taboo, a conscience arises in relation to the taboo itself and the feeling of guilt arises after his violation.

Freud also finds a similarity between the taboo and the symptoms of the obsessional neurosis:

1. The lack of motive for the prohibitions.
2. Their affirmation through internal compulsion.
3. Their ability to shift and to indicate the danger of contagion in contact with the forbidden.
4. The provocation of performance of ceremonial actions, eventuating by the prohibitions.

But it is worth trying to solve the taboo and not only for these reasons. As Freud himself says, "I think every psychological problem deserves an effort to be resolved not only because of itself but also for other reasons. My assumption is that the taboo of the primitive Polynesians is still not as remoted from us as we had assumed in the beginning that the moral and ethical prohibitions to which we obey ourselves are likely to have a fundamental relationship with this primitive taboo and that the elucidation of the taboo could shed light on the vague origin of our own "categorical imperative".

The oldest and most important taboo prohibitions are related to the two basic laws of totemism:
1. Do not kill the totem animal.
2. Do not engage in sexual relations with the worshipers of the same totem.

Proceeding from the fact that there are prohibitions where there are also strong temptations (if there is no strong desire of performing the concrete action, there would be no need for a ban), then we can assume that these two acts are the oldest and strongest temptations of people. But the establishing of the taboo leads to something - the initial desire to perform the forbidden action still exists. It follows from this the appearance of an ambiguous attitude towards the prohibition. On one hand, in the unconscious, people want only to break the prohibitions, but on the other, they are afraid of them and are worried precisely because they want to break them, but fear is stronger than desire. Here, Freud makes a parallel with the neurotic person and says: "But in every particular individual, the desire for this is unconscious, as in the neurotic person."

It is important to pay attention to how to "correct the sin" and what this means about the taboo itself.
Freud says, "If the violation of a taboo can be corrected by redemption or remorse, which in fact is a denial of some welfare or a right, it proves that observance of the taboo prescripts is nothing more than a denial of something highly desirable. Failure to fulfil one denial is replaced by another denial. As for the ceremonial activities associated

with the taboo, we can conclude that remorse precedes purification. "

From what has been said so far, we understand that:

1. The taboo is a long-standing ban imposed on the outside, by some authority, and directed against the strongest human strivings/desires.

2. The desire to transgress the ban continues to exist in the unconscious and it follows from this that the people who obey the taboo have an ambivalent attitude towards the concrete taboo.

3. The magic magnitude attributed to the taboo is derived from the ability to draw people in temptation. It is like an infection because the example is contagious.

4. The redemption of the violated taboo by some refusal shows that in the base of the taboo lies the refusal of something.

As a finale, we will say that the building of psychoanalysis is not built only from clinical cases but from a forest of reliable observations, which, according to Sigmund Freud, are stronger than any experiment. Freud accepts the stories of his patients for scientific data. Everyone can imagine what a great method is the introspection of the couch, free from all limitations and inhibitions. The analytical séance is a scientific method more valuable than the experiment because it is unique by necessity, it is a natural experiment. There are no artefacts, no experience of something that is not in life. Psychoanalysis is defended as a science by the success it achieves.

Analytical Theory. Ideas and Views of Carl Gustav Jung.

Carl Gustav Jung's figure and work are often put on the same level as Freud's. Jung's family comes from Germany, he is a doctor and a psychologist, and his life is flowing in Basil. The portrait created by Sigmund Freud is subject to criticism, disagreement and contradictory assessments, including by his followers and students. The most critical and dramatic is the conflict with Carl Gustav Jung. The year of the critical conflict is 1913.

Carl Gustav Jung has a different point of view on the source and causes of neuroses. According to Freud, the source is the childhood traumas, but according to Jung there are many factors such as misfortune in life, unhealthy human relationships, work failures, and life as a whole, and of course, it does not exclude factors of a sexual nature. Jung does not accept the Oedipus complex by believing that parents are not sexual but moral partners of the child. He does not accept the concept of "sexual energy". He thinks there is a common one which can not be divided. They have a different technique of performing of the seances in particular patient-client physical contact. Freud does not allow it. They also do not share the same view on the interpretation of dreams. But these differences are not the main reason for the separation between them. The big reason is rooted in the different perspectives on the structure of the psyche and the understanding of the nature of the unconscious. For Jung, the psyche is the equivalent of the personality. And this is the reason why two different theories of personality arise.

Jung has ideas on the archetypal appearance of the personality. He talks about "persona" - the mask of the actors with which they play a certain role. He thinks we have an archetype, an unconscious and conscious predisposition to behave in a certain way in different situations and relationships. Personality is understood as a "persona" with the mask that a person puts in to present himself in a particular way that he desires in front of others. He shows an "external personality," and if he becomes obsessed with that personality he becomes a sick person. The point of view of the personality as a "persona" says and suggests a fundamental and undeniable fact that people are personalities when they are adequate to the situation in which they function. The archetypal notion of personality orients towards a perception of personality associated with an adequate human change in a given situation.

Jung talks about the three personality structures:

Personal consciousness - this concept is related to the analysis of the main functions of consciousness such as sensation, thinking, intuition and feelings. This notion describes the man as the holder of conscious functions.

The personal unconscious - this concept refers to the unconscious contents related to the events of the individual life, the personal experience that we have accumulated and pushed/repressed. The personal unconscious is similar in character to the Freud's repressed unconscious, but with a peculiarity, Jung announces that the core of the personal unconscious is "the complex". The complexes are pushed/repressed emotionally saturated contents, complicating our adaptive behaviour.

Collective/universal/generic unconscious - this idea and hypothesis is a central point in the psychological portrayal of the personality and marks the fundamental difference between Sigmund Freud and Carl Gustav Jung regarding the main principle of the psyche. Jung brings out the functioning of psyche from cultural, racial factors with a social nature related to the subject's attitude towards the objects, unlike Sigmund Freud, who brings the functioning of the psyche out of biological factors. Jung believes that in the structure of the human psyche there is a layer, space and judgment that is deepest in the cave, where the experience of all mankind, people of all ages, races, and cultures is postponed; to start with something clear - an experience of how to react, an experience that does not represent knowledge. The collective unconscious is content that is not conscious but influences thoughts, feelings, ideas, and actions. It structures the psyche and behaviour. The collective unconscious is an experience but in a particular form. It is an inherited experience at the neural level of responding in a certain way to significant and recurrent events and objects in our lives. The way of reaction is accomplished as a predisposition, as an instruction we do not realize, as a rule without content, which we apply to the actual content. The collective unconscious has a constructive character in terms of the objective world. These non-content rules correlated and specified to certain objects are called archetypes. These archetypes are revealed in symbols. Archetypal symbols are symbols of the unconscious and are different from the symbols of consciousness.

Jung has explored such archetypes as:
• The most important for of the personality are the "persona", the Self, the shadow;
• The mother;
• The anima and the animus;
• The deities and others.

Jung also makes one of the early typologies of the personality. His typology refers to healthy people but can be used and applied to the sick. These are the phenomena of **"extraversion"** and **"introversion"**. He assumes that the lives of some people are dependent and determined more by the connection with external objects, and the lives of others -

more than the connection with their own experiences and life. Therefore, people have an interaction with two worlds - both external and internal, but each person prefers one of them. **The introvert** disregards from objects, seeks freedom from the outside world, and reduces its significance to its own existence. Jung says: "The standard introvert is characterized by fluctuating reflexivity and endangered nature which is seeking solitary. The introvert preserves himself because of himself. He retires from the objects and always remains in some defensive position". **The extravert** is outwardly oriented. Accepts objects positively. He strives to discover and increase their value. Jung says, "Extraversion is characterized by mobility, open-heartedness, conciliatoriness, living nature, easy adaptability, easily create connections and affection. In the extravert attitude dominates the external factor". The Subject-to-object relation is always a matter of adaptation. Jung says, "It's a fundamental contrast that sometimes turns out to be brighter, sometimes blurred, but always to people with a prominent personality. Extravert and Introvert types are not affected by gender, education, environment, or heredity. They are influenced by the convenience of adaptation". Jung also shows that the functions of the personal consciousness acquire particularities depending on whether we are extraverts or introverts. These two orientations/characteristics such as name and content are used in other theories, mostly dispositions, and their content is expanded. This is based on the clusterization of qualities to a level of generalization.

Jung also develops the **associative experiment** - this method is projective and has unlimited possibilities as long as one knows what to subordinate to. Associative experiments attack the individuality of a person!

A careful look at psychoanalytic theories shows that they give a significant place to the personality as modelled by the unconscious psyche. But this is not all, these theories provoke questions such as **"How conscious is a man and how conscious he is not?"** and also questions are raised such as **"What place has the particular culture, the social and economic structure of society for to the formation of the person?"**

As a conclusion, we will quote Jung's words: "She (psychology) is still in the cradle, and so the time of the generalizing theories has not yet occurred. Even sometimes it seems to me that psychology has not understood either the scale of its tasks or the confusing and complex nature of its subject - the psyche itself "(„About the Foundations of Analytical Psychology" Jung). According to him, her subject matter is maddening!

Individual Psychology. Ideas and Views of Alfred Adler.

Alfred Adler is a member of Freud's Vienna circle and IPA (International Psychoanalysis Association). He is an Austrian doctor and psychologist with high social and civic culture and independence. In 1911, he expressed views other than those of Sigmund Freud and, together with eight other people, the "gang of the ninth" was excluded from the psychoanalytic movement. He takes a standalone path of development and sets the foundations for a movement called **individual psychology**. His views are particularly related to his personal life. He has a traumatic childhood and a later life like this. One morning he finds his brother with whom they are sleeping in the same bed dead. He experiences heavily and suffers a lot because of his qualification of a mentally retarded person when he was in the first grade. Adler graduated excellently medicine at the University of Vienna. In 1920 there was a refusal of having the academical rank to be a professor at the University of Vienna. He graduated in medicine, having at first practice as an ophthalmologist, then as a psychologist.

The disagreement with Sigmund Freud is actually a difference in the main motive of human life. Sigmund Freud puts the sexual motives first, while Adler puts the **social interest**, where the main purpose of life is to acquire status, a position of value among other people, articulated as a **sense of power and superiority**. He raises the slogan "Man has something more than heredity and the environment. He has an artistic or a creative self", which means that he can create himself. The requirements of the environment and human activity develop the person. Alfred Adler is an early harbinger of humanistic psychology. Indivisible, holistic, but he looks at life and concludes and says there are no perfect people. According to him, people have problems, defects, shortcomings. People have a **sense of inferiority or inability** since their childhood. This feeling makes us struggle, make efforts, compensate and overcome the incompleteness. Occasionally, the opposite is the case, a person is making efforts but does not succeed. He may attach an explanatory role to some defect or fault, fixates himself on the defect, and obtain an **inferiority complex**. The complex is something that tortures people. The term was introduced by Carl Gustav Jung. The complex is an experience grouped around an object to which we have a negative feeling. According to Adler, if a person is loved, he gets security from other people, if he is acknowledged, respected if he is valuable to others if he has his own environment for which he is important, he doesn't possess complexes. In his view, the overcoming of these complexes and the acquisition of a sense of authority and superiority make us **healthy people.**

It is important to understand that Adler does not understand superiority as leadership, power, wealth, for him **superiority is upward movement, growth, gaining importance, it is the "great movement upward".** He thinks this feeling is innate. Energy is drawn from the desire to raise. In his look at the person, Adler applies the concept of **lifestyle or vital style.** Every person has his/her **individual line of development**, an individual way to interact with the world and with himself/herself. Vital style fixates **the uniqueness of a person**. It also builds **the biography of a person**. He believes that the explanations for the formation of human character are very naive.

What does human character do?

Adler thinks that the most important factor in the formation of human character is a person's **biography**. Events form the attitude of a person. Personality cannot be seen outside the gained experience. According to Adler, the lifestyle does not have a common pattern of development and is driven by the ultimate goal. The goal is achieved individually, it is formed too early and in the course of life, people can be aware of their defects and compensate them and change them.

Alfred Adler is a figure in the analytical movement that deserves attention not only because he takes a step to the left of Sigmund Freud, but first of all because his point of view for people has original dimensions, both for his time and today. He is also an example of how the personal life of a human, the experience he has acquired can influence the views for the personality. In 1910-1911, he expressed points of view that did not agree with those of Sigmund Freud. In his general orientation towards the person, he realizes a **social approach**. While Sigmund Freud claims that the main motive is sexual interest, Alfred Adler argues that the main motive that guides and structures the lifestyle together with the ultimate goal is the **social interest**, that is, a person in his life strives to achieve a status of value, significance, of acceptance by other people, the status of which the other name is a sense of authority and superiority.

As a citizen and physician Alfred Adler fixates on the obvious fact that there are no perfect people. People have problems, defects, flaws, inconsistencies, and in practice, since childhood, each of us is incomplete. Everyone **has a sense and consciousness of inferiority**, and the desired status of significance makes him struggle, overcome the difficulties and himself and grow. These efforts make sense because Alfred Adler says: "Everyone has the potential for development and a mechanism to develop these potentials. We have more than heredity and the environment. We have a creative self, we can create ourselves, we can cope with the sense of inferiority with its defects. "It may happen that one could fail, doesn't have luck and then asks himself: "Why?" It can attribute an explanatory value to its defect. When the defect begins to torment us, to possess us, to negatively influence the self, the feeling of inferiority has already been transformed into an **inferiority complex**. The complex has conditions to appear. The complex never develops independently of other people, from the environment. If a person is accepted, if he is loved, if he is secure, if he has one to believe in, if he is needed, there is no room for the complex. **Complexes are surmountable on the basis of healthy human relationships.**

Alfred Adler creates a theory called **"Individual Psychology"** that affirms the understanding that each person has his own **lifestyle** and a **final end goal** that structures the style and the whole life. Neuroses, he says, do not come from our sexuality but come and have a reason in the lifestyle, that is, the lonely person is neurotic.

This particular feeling that guides our lives is **the sense of power and superiority**, understood as **connection and acceptance by other people as a conquered individual value and significance**. People are personalities who can compensate for their weaknesses. Alfred Adler met his death in 1937 during lectures.

Neo-Freudianism. Ideas and Views of Erich Fromm and Karen Horney.

The first correction of psychoanalytic theories can be found in neo-Freudians' views, particularly in the views of Erich Fromm, Karen Horney and Harry Sullivan.

Erich Fromm appears on the stage as the founder of a system of views that hit the critical points of the personality. Fromm sociologizes (interprets from a sociological point of view) the psychoanalytic view to man and emphasizes the fact that people are the product of inevitable human relationships. In the formation of the theory of personality, Fromm makes a clash between the cultural and the biological and says that our biological assets must adapt to culture and society. **What is the nature of man?** Nature is the starting point from which personality is defined. To define the nature of man, Erich Fromm gives a meeting of Sigmund Freud and Karl Marx as a non-partisan reading of Marx and says: "Marx has studied the outside nature of the human being, the dependence of man on other people, that is, the dictatorship of society over man, Freud has studied the dependence that comes from within, from the drive. By virtue of this dependence man has a dualistic nature". At the same time, Erich Fromm has a firm social view of the essence of man. Contextually, Erich Fromm reaffirms the idea that personality is the essence of man, that the personality is social and is the connection with the other people. If the essence of the personality is the relationships with other people, then the question arises what the others give to the personality and what the individual give them and how they function as personalities. Every society has created certain economic, political and legal rules of life. Erich Fromm analyzes the life of man from the Middle Ages to the present day, and establishes that for centuries, man has become more and freer, but this freedom has a price - he is losing more and more security for his life. "The only living thing that turns his own existence into a problem is a man." By gaining freedom, but losing security, a person runs away from freedom and seeks a way to find and gain security. Erich Fromm described brilliantly this aspect of the personality through the escape mechanisms:

Authoritarianism, that is, the attempt to join with something that you agree to and obtain security and even power.

Obedience, that is, trying to find security through the obedience of another person. There are also many unconscious motives.

Conformity, that is, trying to find security by changing your own point of view under the pressure of the group.

Fromm concludes that man is lonely and alienated and is under the sign of overcoming this loneliness and alienation. Erich Fromm's views on man and personality are an appeal to a change in the nature of man. He says change can occur when there is a fair, social, economic and moral society, and aggression is caused by the fact that the problems are not solved in the same way for all.

Karen Horney is deeply acquainted with Freudism, a practitioner doctor, a psychotherapist, and a solid theoretical scientist. She takes a look at the personality by analyzing the phenomenon and the concept of "**anxiety**" and, in a sense, by analyzing the concept of **"female psyche"**. She creates a simple, understandable, trustworthy personality orientation of anxiety-related people by defining **three types of personalities** that every psychotherapist works without even knowing. The main concept in Horney's theory of personality is the notion of **"basal anxiety"**. Anxiety is one of the phenomena in the structure of the psyche. Eventually, people are divided into calm and worried/anxious. Anxiety is a state in which a person experiences himself as useless, scared of life/being, despising himself, hostile to others and to the world and as self-denying. Roughly speaking, here thinking is distorted, in principle rejecting. The anxious person has a need to connect with other people, from love, recognition, independence, and coping with problems. The anxious people carry low self-esteem and, in this sense, this is not adequate. There is also a fixation on how they see other people. Karen Horney has a definite advantage in understanding this phenomenon. She makes a psychographic/psychobiographical analysis of anxiety and starts from the fact that young children experience their connection with their parents as physical and mental dependence. If a child lives in a normal atmosphere, a little major but not hysterical, things are fine. If, however, the atmosphere is unhealthy, traumatic - the child is experiencing himself/herself as frightened, vulnerable. Here, says Horney, basal anxiety appears. The child experiences himself/herself a discarded, useless, gotten into an irrational world. The rejected person, the rejected child is anxious, hates his parents, but is weak and can not punish them. Anxiety is an experience, a state and a trait that shapes every expression of a person.

Anxiety is a consequence of:
1. Alienation by parents;
2. Lack of parents;
3. Excessive control;
4. A hostile atmosphere in which the child lives (maltreatment, beating);
5. Discrimination/neglecting especially in the conditions of several children;
6. A great admiration directed at the child;
7. Excessive love for the child;

There is **physiological anxiety** associated with the physiological needs associated with whether they are satisfied or not and the **psychic anxiety** that arises in relation to the adequacy of the Self-image. There is a difference in knowing who you are in relation to the attitude towards this knowledge. In some people this is adequate and critical, in others it is inadequate and uncritical.

What personal orientations are observed?

Compliant personality - Orientation Towards People - the behaviour of this type of personality is characterized by indecision, helplessness and dependence. This type says, "Ah, how poor and unhappy I am." A person is aware of the need for a partner, friend, spouse, guide, beloved, or relationship. The pursuit of this strategy aims to reduce tension, to reach safety and security. The slogan of these people is, "If I comply, they will not disturb me, they will not bother me." The compliant person mentally wants to be loved, accepted, protected and guided, to be necessary, not isolated. This is a survival strategy, and here is often discussed whether there is no hidden masochism and whether behind this culturally justified servility is hidden concealed aggression. This personality has low self-esteem, plays the role of being weak and unhappy. Sexual acts are passive. Here is a manifestation of the evolutionary reaction **obedience**.

Aggressive Personality - Orientation Against People - The slogan of this type of personality is "I have power, no one can push me. Life is a struggle of everyone against everyone. What is important is what I get - money, power, love, idea, it does not matter." This type of personality acts tactical and amicable in the name of the benefit (utilitarian types). Narcissistic, in love with himself, idealizes his image. Haughty, vengeful, proud, strong, leader and guide. Perfectionist, oriented to high standards he chooses the best if he is the one who chooses. The needs of this type of personality are to be the first, to always win, to have a reputation, to be respected and accepted. These people are instrumental, users, they use the others. The main orientation of this type is power over the surroundings. Here is a manifestation of the evolutionary **battle** reaction.

Withdrawing personality - **Orientation From People** - the attitude of this type of personality is "I do not care; if I exclude myself and if I suspend myself, everything will be fine." Here acts the evolutionary regimes and **escaping** reactions. These people do not invest themselves. They are relieved of involvement. They are self-sufficient.

They discover everything in themselves. They move in indifferently and evenly, superficially, have no affinity for emotional experiences. They are focused on solitude and do not solve basal anxiety through power or love. They protect their own private life. Many withdrawing types are artists and their isolation is a comfortable condition. The main tendency is that they seek and discover everything in themselves.

All three strategies are aimed at reducing the sense of anxiety that arises from social relationships. The healthy person, unlike the neurotic, uses all three strategies, combines them and adapts successfully. The neurotic one works with one of the strategies, fixates on it, and treats negatively the other strategies.

Stages of Psychosocial Development of Personality - Erik Erikson.

*I*t must be borne in mind that the birth of a person does not coincide with the birth of the personality. A person possesses the characteristics of the species to which he belongs, but he becomes a personality is in the process of his development.

What matters is the social environment in which the child grows - family, school, peers, friends. Quite often arises the question from what age it can be considered that begins the fastest building of personality. This is the age at which the child learns very actively the language, begins to understand that it can manifest autonomy and activity by itself. It can also independently move in space and provide things for food, play, or other activity. The most important education during this period is the fact that the child realizing his or her activity starts to use the pronoun "I". In an attempt to determine stages in personality development, it appears that there are some differences in the periodization of the life course. It should be borne in mind that the criteria that are used as the basis of periodization are the factors that influence the psychological development during a certain age period. One of the most frequently quoted and popular contemporary theories about the overall development of life course is the theory of Erik Erikson. It is based on the

epigenetic principle that, from birth to death, a person passes through genetically predetermined stages, experiencing **8 psychosocial crises** that are specific to each age (crisis - opportunity/danger). The outcome of these crises may be auspicious to the future development of the personality or it may be unfavourable. Each subsequent stage is based on the development results of the previous stages. Achieving the **"I" identity** during adolescence is central to his concept of development. Formation of identity involves, on the one hand, the synthesis and the only previous experience and development of the child and on the other hand, provides the basis for its future progressive development as a mature person. A sense of identity means perceiving yourself as something complete, as well as awareness of the continuity of one's own experience. Erik Erikson believes that the development of the personality is justified by the interaction of three main factors - the individual-biological, the upbringing and the socio-cultural environment.

8 stages of development and the crisis:

The essence of the first crisis is expressed in trust/mistrust.
The person experiences it in the first year after birth. The decisive factor for human development during this period is whether the caregivers satisfy him or do not meet his physiological needs. If these needs are met, the child develops a sense of basic trust in the world around, and if they are not satisfying, a sense of mistrust develops. This stage is also associated with virtue and hope, belief in the attainment of the most important desires despite the difficulties. This faith is passed on from mother to child.

The second crisis is defined as autonomy against doubt and shame.

It is experienced by a person from 1 to 3 years of age. During this period, the child's first attempts are made to be trained in particular to comply with the social requirements for self-control and regulation of his / her bodily functions (toilet/potty training). If parents are attentive to the child and patiently help them develop their ability to control body functions, the child develop a sense of autonomy, for self-management. The other way round is too strict or inconsistent parental control can create a sense of shame and doubt in the child, which is related to the fear of losing control of the organism. The sense of self-control without loss of respect is the first source of a feeling of free will.

The third crisis is related to the fight of the initiative against guilt.

From 3 to 6 years of age. During this period the self-assertion of the child begins to develop as the child actively begins to explore and intervene in the environment in which he/she operates. Children constantly create plans in their games and their implementation leads to building a sense of initiative. Conversely, experiencing failures and irresponsibility can lead to building obedience and sense of guilt. The main input of the stage of the initiative for the later development of identity consists in building a sense of purpose or the courage to pursue personally significant goals, regardless of the risks and possible failure.

The fourth crisis is connected with the fight of diligence/industry against the feeling of inferiority.
From 7 to 12 years of age. While the rest of the three periods, the main social environment in which crises are resolved

is home and family, now during this fourth stage, the crisis takes place in a new environment (the school). The child learns to work and this is his preparation for solving future social tasks. Depending on the situation in the school environment, the methods of education and upbringing in children build a "taste for labour" - the assiduousness/diligence/industry or vice versa, the sense of inferiority. The sense of inferiority can also manifest in terms of school tasks, but also in terms of the place the child takes among her friends.

The fifth crisis is expressed as a fight of the identity against diffusion (role confusion).

Covers the period of adolescence 13-15 years old (the first stages of the crisis). This is the culmination of Eric Erickson's theory, as during this period adolescents synthesize their previous experiences to form a stable sense of identity. For example, from the first stage to the crisis of identity comes the need for self-trust and trust in the others, which is why the adolescents are very "starving" for looking for people and ideas to believe in. During the second stage of the crisis (16-18 years of age), if it is built a feeling that one can freely define oneself through what he/she wants, then the adolescent starts looking for an opportunity to make decisions about his future professional activity (professional identity). Achieving identity by answering the question of "Who am I?" Is also accompanied by the virtue generated at this stage, that is, the ability to maintain engagement despite contradictory value systems.

The sixth crisis is defined as intimacy against isolation.

These are the problems of early maturity (20 to 40 years of age). The main thing during this period is the search for closeness with a loved one with whom life is shared, and in the event that the attempt to find such a person is unsuccessful, a sense of isolation begins to manifest. Identity during this period is expressed as, "We are what we love," and love is the quality that is strongest during this period.

The seventh crisis is determined by resolving the collision of generativity against stagnation.

From 40 to 60 years of age. The time during which the main efforts of a person are directed to the care for the next generation. The period is characterized by high productivity in creativity in various forms of life. But if one can not create a generation and take care of it, then regression, a sense of stagnation, boredom and interpersonal impoverishment arise. During this stage is built the virtue of care and love.

The eighth crisis is defined as the fight of ego integrity against despair.
It comes after 60 years of age. The time when a man realises and accepts his life path and the people he was with during that time. That gives him a feeling of wholeness and integrity. If one does not accept his destiny, if he is indignant at the events and with the people in his life, this leads to the appearance of a sense of despair. It is expressed in the fact that the time is too short to try to start another life on other paths to pursue integrity. The virtue that arises during this period is wisdom. The wise man accepts the fact that his own life had gone exactly the way it should. In this way, he faces the end of his life with the thought "I am what will survive from me".

Jean Piaget and cognitive development during childhood.

Researchers are trying to answer questions like "When do children start seeing things from another perspective when they start to think logically and abstractly?", or like "How does the child's mind develop?" and others. Jean Piaget, whose interests in the area date back to the 1920s when he worked in Paris and explores the intelligence of children, was also looking for answers to such questions.

To this end, he constructed tests with questions, but unlike the traditional approach oriented to children's achievements analysis, Jean Piaget was interested in the question "Why do children give wrong answers?" While in this fact other researchers saw childhood mistakes, he was able to track how intelligence works because he found that children's mistakes of the same age were similar. Jean Piaget's researches lasted for about 50 years, where he found that the mind of the child should not be seen as a miniature model of the mind of adults because small children understand the world in a different way than adults. Jean Piaget finds that the child's mind is going through certain stages of development, which lie between the simple reflexes of the newborn and the abstract thinking of the adult. For example, an 8-year-old child compares things that a 3-year-old child cannot. According to Jean Piaget, the driving force of intellectual development is one's desire to understand, to examine his experience. This is why the developing brain builds concepts that Jean Piaget calls "schemas." According to him, "schemas" can be defined as "mental molds" in which people pour their experience. In this way, by adulthood, one has built up a myriad of "schemes" that are ranked or arranged in some order. To better explain how someone creates and uses his own "schemas," Jean Piaget introduces 2 concepts - "ASSIMILATION" and "ACCOMMODATION." According to him, a person interprets his experience according to his current or actual state. People use "schemas" to include, that is, to assimilate new experiences. ASSIMILATION is the process of incorporating new information as a relevant part of an individual's already existing cognitive "schemas". At the same time, people can adjust their "schemas" by ACCOMMODATING them to modulate new experiences. With the term "ACCOMMODATION", Jean Piaget refers to the process of changing existing mental structures to integrate new and old experiences.

Stages of cognitive development according to Jean Piaget

According to Jean Piaget, the process of the development of intelligence is as follows. "Schemas" or ways of processing knowledge are organized into operations. Different combinations correspond to qualitatively different stages of cognitive growth. The stages change into an INVARIANT SEQUENCE, which means that every normal child has to go through different stages, and each subsequent phase arises from the achievements of the previous stage. The new and more adaptive cognitive abilities integrate the previous ones and transform them into more sophisticated mental structures. The transition from one stage to another means a qualitative and fundamental transformation of the individual ways of constructing and interpreting the surrounding world. Although the sequence of the stages is immutable and universal, there may still be individual differences in the speed and rate of passage through the stages, and therefore age limits can only be determined approximately.

Sensorimotor stage - from birth to 1.5 - 2 years of age.

During this period, children acquire knowledge of the world through various actions (trial and error), based on which purposeful sensory and motor actions are developed. The end of this period is characterized by the fact that the child can imitate the actions of others, but also reaches new ways of acting by combining previously acquired knowledge and "schemas". For this short period from birth to the second year, the child moves from a state which is highly dependent on reflexes and heredity to a conscious individual capable of thinking with symbols.

Preoperational stage - from 2 to 7 years of age.

During this stage, children already formulate concepts and use symbols such as the language. These concepts are limited by their personal and immediate experience. During this stage, the perceptions of cause and effect are very limited and children have difficulty classifying objects and events.

Concrete operational stage - from 7 to 11,12 years of age.

During this stage, children begin to think logically, to classify objects by several signs, and to operate with mathematical concepts. At this stage, children reach an understanding of the storage of objects. According to Jean Piaget, this is a major achievement at the concrete operational stage. The child is capable to judge changes in the number of substances by relying on his or her logical thinking, not just the data of the sensory perception.

To illustrate this phenomenon, Jean Piaget creates a famous experiment to test the phenomenon of storage. Children are shown two identical glasses with equal amounts of water. After the child agrees that the amount of water is the same, the water from the first glass is poured into the other, which is higher and narrower, then the question is asked "How much water is there in the higher glass? Has the water become more or less in it in comparison with the first glass, or has the amount remained the same? ' Most of the children who

 are around the age of 6 years claim that in the tall glass of water there is more quantity than in the shorter. Even after they have seen that the water pours from the short in the tall glass, they continue to claim that there is more quantity in the tall glass of water. This experiment had been repeating with children from different cultures and the results are all the same. Jean Piaget concludes that until the third stage, children form judgments which in large part are based on perceptual rather than logical processes. In other words, they rather believe their eyes than logic. Children of later age in the concrete operational stage do not base their judgments solely on perceptions but begin to use logic. When children demonstrate such capability, psychologists claim that they already have access to the concept of "CONSERVATION". The term "CONSERVATION" was introduced by Jean Piaget to refer to the process of awareness by the child that the physical properties of substances - volume, weight, quantity, remain constant regardless of changes in their form and appearance.

Formal operational stage - from 12,13 to the end of puberty.

The rising generation can analyze when solving logical problems, both with specific and abstract content. They can systematically consider all possibilities, make plans for their future, think by analogy or by metaphors.

Lawrence Kohlberg and the moral development of the personality.

*T*o study how moral development of children progresses, the American psychologist Lawrence Kohlberg decides to conduct a study in 1958. Morality refers to the unwritten rules that determine how we should treat others and how we evaluate the behaviour of others. To this end, he presents several moral/ethical dilemmas and presents them to 75 girls and boys of different ages, listening carefully to their opinions. He is less interested in the answers given by children, such as "it is right" or "not", but rather in the arguments they used to defend their opinion. Depending on the explanation given by the children, **Kohlberg determines 3 levels/stages in moral development:**

Pre-Conventional - Characteristic for children between 4 and 10 years. Judgments at this level are determined by arguments related to external circumstances and the views of others are not taken into account. It is divided into 2 stages:

• **Stage 1 - "Obedience and punishment orientation".** During this stage, children are oriented toward the consequences of the action, not the analysis of the motives or causes of the action. In their view, good behaviour is not punishable.

• **Stage 2 - "Self-interest orientation".** In this case, the arguments are determined according to the personal benefit that can be derived from the act. It becomes clear that people are of value only when they are of interest to the person doing the deed.

Conventional - applies to children between 10 and 13 years old. This is a period in which they are oriented towards other people's opinions and judgment. This level covers stages 3 and 4:

• **Stage 3** - the **"Good child"** or orientation toward the approval of others. Children view behaviour as good if it pleases others and is associated with approval. Assessment here includes both the evaluation of consequences and the evaluation of intentions.

• **Stage 4** - "**Authority and social-order maintaining orientation**" - during this stage, children's judgments are based on authority and laws. Behaviour is rated as good if it complies with these norms.

Post-Conventional - develops after the age of 13 and, according to Kohlberg, this is the level of true morality, and it is judged by behaviour based on one's own criteria, which implies high mental development. The two stages are:

• **Stage 5 - "Social contract and democracy orientation"** - justification for the action is made based on respect for a democratically-made decision or respect for human rights in general. Here, the value of the individual is determined by the human rights that presuppose the equality of all people, regardless of what personal or business relationship they find with each other. In certain circumstances, one may decide to violate the law to save the other.

• **Stage 6** - **"Stage of orientation toward universal principles"** - a deed is classified as correct if it is dictated by conscience, regardless of the legitimacy or opinion of others, or in other words, human life is valuable in itself and there should be no reason to violate this universal principle.

Attachment theory. Basic concepts and styles of attachment.

Creating and maintaining close relationships of affection and intimacy is an important task at an early age. Attachment is defined as "relationships characterized by strong interdependence, intense mutual feelings and vital emotional contacts."

Adults usually look for two types of interpersonal relationships:
1. Close, dyadic relationships of emotional attachment to another person who is special for us as an intimate romantic friend, husband.

2. Establishing and maintaining social connections in broader social networks or affiliation groups (formal or informal).

In recent years, more and more researchers have become interested in the impact of early attachment (parent-child) styles on the development of close life-long relationships. **There are two opposite hypotheses in this regard:**
1. According to the first hypothesis, one believes that there are direct continuity and permanence of the parenting style of affection in the later intimate and mostly in romantic relationships.
2. The other hypothesis claims that there is a change in the early attachment styles in the context of the close adult relationships which are new in content and purposes.

The theoretical framework of attachment research is based on the

research of John Bowlby and Mary Ainsworth.

Attachment theory maintains the theses that the desire of human beings to create satisfying and affective relationships with the significant others has a fundamental adaptive and developmental function. According to Bowlby, attachment is a major genetic need and goal in human survival and development. He views the attachment in general as an evolutionary mechanism for survival in both animals and humans. According to him, through this attachment mechanism, newborns are providing themselves care and protection from their caregivers, and therefore early parent-child interactions are very important for child development. These relationships set the first framework through which individuals are going to perceive themselves and others. According to

Bowlby's theory, people in their social relations with others naturally create internal affective and cognitive models both for themselves and for the typical traits of interaction with the significant others.

These internal or operational models are thought to organize the development of the individual and manage his or her social behaviour. According to him, the main research problem is the problem of how and why newborns attach themselves emotionally to the people who care for them and experience emotional depression when physically separated from them. He maintains the thesis that the emotional attachment system, composed of a specific emotional and behavioural mechanism, is designed to keep children physically close to their parents. According to him, this system of attachment is common to human species and animals and was probably selected during evolutionary development. When they remain in close contact with their parents, who protect them from danger, the young who have these attachment mechanisms are more likely to survive to reproductive age, to reproduce and pass on those mechanisms to future generations. Bowlby supports the hypothesis that individual differences in the emotional and behavioural mechanisms of attachment formed in childhood remain relatively stable throughout life. Operational models of attachment can be differentiated by two intersecting polar axes.

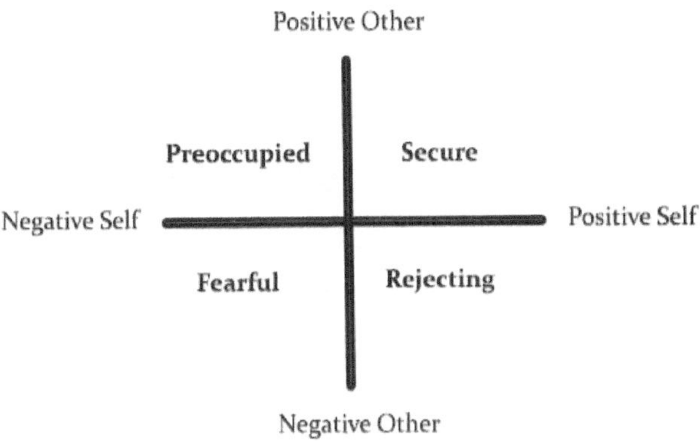

On the Horizontal axis, on the left, is the Negative Self and on the left is the Positive Self. On the top is Positive Other, and below is a Negative Other.
In the first quadrant, on the upper left, is Preoccupied. Between Positive Other and Positive Self stands Secure. Bottom left is the place of the Fearful. And lastly, between the Positive Self and the Negative Other is the Rejecting.

In his research, Bowlby monitors infants and young children and systematizes

three types of reactions when separating the child from its object of attachment:
1. Protest - crying, clinging to the object of attachment and inability to calm the child by other persons.
2. Despair - sadness and passive behaviour of the child.
3. Alienation - the active avoidance of the parent upon his or her return.

Children who successfully reconnect with the parent when return see him or her as a source of security, safety and peace of mind.
Mary Ainsworth's cross-cultural studies show that the need for attachment is universal for all cultures, regardless of social and economic status.

A three-category model of early attachment. Mary Ainsworth.

Empirical studies that rely on attachment theory focus mainly on the differentiation of various attachment styles. Based on modelling the situation of separation with the mother, Mary Ainsworth identifies three main styles of attachment and three types of emotional distress in physical separation with the object of attachment. The design of the study is known as a "strange situation" - the child enters the toy room and stays alone for a while, then an unknown person enters, the mother goes out and the child stays alone, after a while the mother returns to the room.

Typical features and the relative share of attachment styles found in a distress situation are:

1. **Safe style** - children successfully perceive the parent as safe support and a source of safety when in a state of distress. They are sociable, they explore the situations, they are friendly to strangers, they show anger and sadness at their mother's departure, but they adapt to her absence and are easily comforted. When she returns, they are happy and quickly accept her again.

2. **Anxious (ambivalent) style** - These children mix affection behaviours and open outbursts of protest and anger when in distress. Rather, they are frightened by the presence of the

stranger, when they part with their mother they cling to her and do not calm down easily. They show a mix of searching for closeness and annoyance at the mother's return.

3.   **Avoiding attachment style** - Characterizes children who, in distress, avoid the parent and demonstrate alienation. They seem independent and confident, but there is a deliberate avoidance of the mother figure. When the mother goes out, they are reserved and avoid the stranger person.

What are the mothers of children with different types of attachment?
1. Mothers of safe-style children feel comfortable in physical contact with the child and are sensitive to their needs.
2. Mothers of anxious-style children are insensitive to their needs or inconsistent

in their care. Sometimes too anxious and sometimes ignorant.

3. Avoiding style mothers of children feel uncomfortable with physical contact with the child, tend to be irritable to the child, and are not sensitive to the kid's needs.

A four-category model of adult attachment styles. Bartholomew and Horowitz.

This model operationalizes most precisely John Bowlby's idea of attachment as an internal, mental and affective model of the relationship of the Me-The other. Below are presented the analogues of the four Bartholomew and Horowitz styles and the three styles differentiated for the early attachment.

1. **A Secure attachment style** corresponds to the Secure attachment from the three-category model of early

attachment. People with this style have positive values in both dimensions of the internal operating models - they feel comfortable with both intimacy and independence. They develop mental models of themselves in which they perceive themselves as friendly, good-natured and liked. They perceive the significant others as well-meaning, trustworthy people. They are not afraid of commitment and feel good about being dependent on each other. They are capable of giving and receiving support and easily draw closer. They keep positive memories of their childhood and describe their parents as benevolent and punitive only as a last resort. They have confidence in social situations, increased willingness to get to know others and more openness, which facilitates reciprocity in relationships. Their positive self-esteem is based on successful relationships with others. They feel loved, supported and cared for by their partners. They believe there is someone to rely on when needed.

2. **A Preoccupied attachment style** corresponds to the Anxious (ambivalent) style of early attachment during childhood. People with this style have a negative model for themselves and a positive one for the others. These are individuals filled with a strong drive to make connections and extremely affectionate in social contacts. They are perceived as misunderstood, insecure and subordinate in close relationships. At the same time, they perceive significant others as unreliable and unwilling to engage in lasting relationships. The preoccupied people want to be completely emotionally close to their partners but worried that the others do not want to get involved with them to the point of complete merging with one

another (which is their aim). They share about fickle parents who were both authoritarian and benevolent, sending contradictory messages of love and rejection. These individuals doubt their own worth and value, and therefore stubbornly seek from others confirmation, support and positive feedback. Hence, their self-confidence varies dramatically depending on the perception of approval or rejection by the others. They describe themselves as emotional, jealous and with hot temper.

3. **Fearful attachment style** - consistent with the Avoiding attachment style. People with this style have negative cognitive and emotional patterns for themselves as well as for the others. They avoid dependence and feel good when they are not in a close relationship. Avoiding attachment is due to their fear of being hurt. They perceive their parents

as rejecting, authoritarian and malicious. These people desire closeness to others but are filled with convictions that they are not loved and of no personal significance to anyone. They have negative beliefs about others and perceive them as rejecting and unceremonious. They cannot reveal themselves and rely on others. They are capable of displaying malice and jealousy in romantic relationships.

4. **Dismissing style of attachment** - there is no analogue of the three-category model. People with this attachment style have a positive model for themselves and a negative for others. They avoid affection for fear of losing their independence and identity. They describe their parents as unreliable, irresponsible, authoritarian and malicious. Deprived of love and affection in their childhood, they have adopted a

strategy to control the stress of a lack of attachment while distrusting others and maintaining emotional distance. They show less interest in forming close relationships and value their self-confidence, independence and competence without relying on others for support. They claim that they have never fallen in love, almost never reveal themselves, and more often establish casual sexual relations with casual partners as a way of avoiding intimacy. They may be gentle or emotionally expressive, hostile, cold and distant from other people.

Motivation and personality.

The motive category is fundamental to the psychology of personality. There is a hidden tendency for the personality to be reduced to motivation, and justly, motives are perceived as the core of the personality. The greatest credit for the introduction of the term motive in psychology was given by Kurt Lewin and Sigmund Freud. By introducing the term motive, they reveal the complexity of a person's mental life.

The term motive comes from the Latin "movero", which means push, direct, drive, steer.
In connection with this etymology, there is a brief definitive understanding of the

motive known as the 'impetus for action'. Such a definition of motive is not untrue, but it is quite a high school, incomplete and inaccurate. This definition identifies only one function of the motive, and this is the so-called "stimulus function". The phenomenon and the concept of "motive" are covered by the phenomenon and the concept of "psychic reason", that is to say - material reworked from the psyche and consciousness. All too often, the concept of "external motivation" is also found in some factors. The phenomena of the psyche are internal! The motive, if it is psychic, could no be external.

The motive is this psychic fact (need, feeling, conviction, value) that explains to us why and in the name of what we are acting. If we accept this understanding, we, therefore, accept the most essential function of the motive, the "meaning-forming." A motive function can perform various psychic contents and the definition of a motive is attributed to the role they play. Motives are different from stimuli and are often processing of the stimulus. "Intelligence tells us how to act, and the motive - why we act."

Kurt Lewin differentiates 3 types of motive:
1. Ground for action/formation of cause.
2. Object - what the action is directed at.
3. Regulation of behaviour to the target and tension is reduced to 0.

The essence of motives is best revealed in their essential functions:

1. **Stimulus Function** - It is thought to be a basic function, but it is good to know that it is one of the main functions. If there is a motive, then it actually drives action. If a person needs to develop and

grow, to achieve competence, that need compels him to learn.

2. **Energetic function** - motives give power to thought and behaviour, initiate activity, and in principle, there is no activity without motive.

3. **"Meaning-forming"** function - the most important! It explains not only the value of the object to which the behaviour is directed but also the importance of action for the person himself. Awareness of the meaning of what it gives us. The global urge to find meaning and discover the meaning of something is the strongest side of motives. The meaning-forming function of a motive is highly integrated with the level of personality development. Attributing meaning is not an arbitrary and uncontrollable process and, in many cases, marked.

Specific motives (for specific behaviour) are most difficult to diagnose. There are many complex metamorphoses in a particular motivation. All functions of the motive are organized around a meaning-forming function.

4. **Rehabilitation/justification function** - in this function, the motive also has unconscious components. The motives also have the function of justifying the person, of misrepresenting things, and of incorporating some additional circumstance. It is difficult to assess how this additional circumstance changes the real motive and to what extent. This function is expressed in search of a sense of justice, innocence, chance.

Motives are not traits, they are not dispositions, and speaking of **dispositional motives** is quite elusive (the motive follows from our extroversion or consciousness). But traits may help to shape the motives. One is a trait, another is a personal disposition. The trait applies to all people.

Situational motives - motives generated by a particular situation. It's not a good concept, but situations indeed provoke a certain type of motivation.

Character.

The notion and the term "character" belongs in the language of the average person without being clear about what content is included in it. The term is also used by other sciences such as literature, ethics, etc. It is present in propaganda, and generally in the social sciences. Satisfactory psychological thinking always associates character with personality, and in the strict sense of the word, it is an individual typological property of personality. Broadly speaking, the terms "character" and "personality" are 80% the same, especially if the personality is interpreted as structured by traits or dispositions.

The thesis that character does not tell us about a person's social value is difficult to prove especially when we refer to **Erich Fromm's teaching on the social type of character**. This teaching reveals exactly this side of the character - how valuable one person is to others and which type of character has low social value. The value of a character is reflected both in its functions and in its content.

The character has both functional and content characteristics. These characteristics raise the question **"Where does the content of the character come from - a person's inheritance or social experience?"** The truth is that the same experience we acquire can be individualized by both biological and specific mental characteristics.

Even in ancient Greece, the seal was the mark by the master put on the goods he produces, and in this sense, the seal is a symbol of individuality

and of something typical, something sustainable (sustainability). Even Aristotle speaks of "etos."

Character is an individual combination and integration of essential personality traits that formulate a sustainable attitude of man towards reality and the world. This sustainable attitude is manifested through behaviour. In this sense, the character is also a behavioural program for the implementation of a behaviour.

According to **Alfred Adler**, the "character is a certain position, a way in which one approaches his environment. A guiding line in realizing his pursuit of meaningfulness in close connection with the sense of community. "

The dictionary definition of character is the individual combination of resistant mental characteristics of a person, which determines typical behaviours in certain situations and circumstances.

The delicate moment is that the character marks not so much what we do, but how we do it, how durable it is and how typical it is for us.

Typical / character methods of reaction are manifested and are dependent / conditioned on the mental reality to which they are related. A characteristic reaction can be typified by our intelligence, willpower, morality or temperament.

In the structure of the character, global psychic characteristics are present and give a certain nuance, a certain personality of the character.

It is not difficult to find individuals who are typically taking action by subjecting them to deep mental processing. Thus we can conditionally speak of a **rational type of character**, of a person who relates to the world after always using intellectual self-control.

Irrational type of character - it is spontaneous, emotional, etc. Some individuals typically can neglect intellectual control and blindly subject to impulses, drives, momentary conveniences, and act in an affectively deterministic way.

It is difficult to subtract morality from the character structure because we can think about what we want, but we cannot do everything we want because behaviour affects other people.

The character can be defined partly as **moral and immoral**, with justice being seen as the 'criterion' for that.

The temperament is also present in the structure of the character, especially in his behavioural side. It is not difficult to notice that some people react slowly, calmly, by implication, they are inert; others react explosively, uncontrollably, violently, it is typical to be reactive. Temperament gives dynamics and some kind of external appearance to the character.

Willpower plays an extremely important function in the character structure. Will plays the role of soldering material; it is the cement of character architecture and one can confidently speak of **volitional and involuntary character**. Will is an indicator of a developed personality, a ceiling for human development.

Typical volitional behaviour lends value to the character and underlies general mental development, which science has not yet explained well.

With the power of will, there is an overcoming of difficulties and problems. There is an accumulation of experience in the dissatisfactions, sufferings, trials. People of volitional nature successfully overcome difficult and critical situations. Attempts to make a typology of the human character are unsuccessful! Most of the attempts coincide with the typologies of personality or neuroticism, and it is difficult to speak because there is a mismatch in the extravert and introvert type of character (such character cannot be defined).

For the honour of psychology, some contribution to the typology of character and in general to character doctrine was made by Erich Fromm.

According to **Erich Fromm** the term "social character" was introduced, as was the term "attitude" for the first time by English psychologist Herbert Spencer. Erich Fromm extends the content of this concept and makes a typology of characters.

Sigmund Freud tries to explain the character through the "libido theory" - he thinks that blocked sexual energy sublimates in another action.

Erich Fromm makes a breakthrough in the field and thinks that social character is a projection of the culture, economic and political structure of society.

According to Sigmund Freud and Erich Fromm, there are usually 2 types of character, for which the 2 basic instincts stand, respectively:
1. **Biophilic Character** - Finds expression as good that serves life. Love for life and other people.
2. **Necrophilic character** - a tendency to the death, destruction, crushing, denying and pushed/repressed.

Only Erich Fromm views man as a concrete historical being, not as an abstract one.
On the one hand, it is thought that man has an innate nature of the character, and society is created to satisfy that nature (man to survive and develop). Yes,

but there are needs in the essential nature of man. To this day, no society has emerged to meet everyone's needs.

In every society, the individual characters of people are different. At the same time, if we neglect these individual characters, we find, if not all, large groups of people who possess character traits generated and relevant/corresponding to the society itself. A system of characteristics called the "social type of character". The social character is an essential element in the functioning of society. Due to this nature, the economic structure of society is connected with the ideas prevailing in it.

Erich Fromm - "By the term 'social character', I mean the core of the character structure, inherent of the majority of the representatives of a certain culture, opposite to the individual character, which makes people different from each other."

The type is based on common, same features. The social character can only be understood in relation to its role and function.

The main function of the social character is to shape/build and direct human efforts and actions in the name of preserving this society. It has nothing to do with our inheritance. It is an individualized social tendency to maintain the structure of society. The social character marks and embodies the prescriptions of society to the individual and to the patterns of his behaviour that strengthen the society itself.

Erich Fromm typifies first of all 2 types of character:
1. Unproductive
2. Productive

By structuring them into 5 character types or 5 orientation types:

1. Receptive Character Type/Receptive Orientation
2. Selfish Type/Orientation (Exploitative Character Type)
3. Hoarding Character Type/Orientation (Hamster / Accumulating)
4. Marketing Character Type/Orientation
5. Productive Character Type/Orientation

Roughly speaking, these types of character can be correlated with a particular type of society:
1. Slavery
2. Feudal and totalitarian
3. Early, startup capitalism
4. Market economy
5. Utopian-humanistic society.

Features of different types/orientations:

1. **Receptive Type** - all goods and values are out of man. His behaviour is directed

to receive/take (money, belongings, pleasure from the outside). The external source is important! His thesis is "you want to be loved but you may not love". These people do not generate ideas and values, they are self-paralyzing in character. If they are religious, they expect everything from God. Thankful and loyal to those who support them. Emotionally dependent, they have oral traits (suck from others) and are predominant type in times of poverty.

2. **Exploitative Type** - the source of values is out of it, but receives/takes with force, violence, cunning, does not wait to receive, but takes. The orientation of these types applies to every sphere of life. The methods are capturing, appropriation, conquest, plagiarism. A distinctive feature - they are not constructive, they do not create. The things they take are always better and

more valuable than what they create. They want to take the more valuable thing they see in the others. They love the stolen, they love the types who offer themselves. They are also social kleptomaniacs with a tendency to take without having need. The main attraction is to take away from others thinking that the better is there. They are cynical, suspicious, jealous and they do not appreciate what they have.

3. **Hoarding/Accumulating Type** - the tendency to store, accumulate, preserve makes a person calm. This is an enemy of wastefulness and is very distrustful. They have a distrust of what is outside of them. They want the alien, they don't give theirs. They are tidy, silent, neat, fanatically pure, they think the world is unclean. They want to be saved from the outside. The thesis is - "there is nothing new under the sun". They have a fear of

intimacy, they are suspicious, pathological enemies of stealing and deprivation.

4. **Marketing Type** - the centres around which the character and behaviour of these people are built are:
• **The benefit**
• **The profit**
• **Buying and selling**

Erich Fromm said, "the whole world has become the object of purchase, not just the objects." They are selling conscience - the cost depends on the profit.

Thomas Hobbes has said - "A man is a wolf to another man".

These people perceive themselves as a commodity, they identify with the price and the money they receive.

All these 4 types are unproductive! These orientations do not exist independently, they are not separated. Receptive type can be combined with marketing type. According to Erich Fromm, social life conditions determine which orientation will dominate!

5. **Productive Orientation** - refers to the formation of the type of character that produces human essence (justice, morality, responsibility, human solidarity). Non-productive orientations do not produce economic and moral solidarity. Such a person has not been created yet and his creation implies another social and economic system, another type of attitude. The productive man is nowadays the unrealistic/utopian ideal of a humanistic view, and above all of the ideas of a possible change in the nature of man.

The needs.

The fundamental position from which we should start is that all living systems are active. Activity connects them to the internal and external environment and leads to changes that sustain life, make life possible within certain limits. This condition that makes life possible is called homeostasis (a state of equilibrium between the internal and external environment that ensures survival, adaptation, reproduction and development). The fact that relates to the essence of the needs is that every living organism permanently, constantly or cyclically experiences lack/deficit of living conditions (food, water, housing, love, self-representation, etc.) but depends on the complexity of the living system. Lack/deficiency of living conditions is a state that can be conscious, experiencing and this experience is called a need.

Need is a psychic experience of mismatch/dissonance between internal and external living conditions. "Need is a specific essential force in living organisms that provides a link to the reality of self-preservation and self-development. To be precise, the need is the necessity for something that lies outside the organism - there is always an object." Needs have objective character, and the object may be material and ideal. Needs have a signalling function. This feature could inform the person of something, and the most widespread in form and expression is tension and suffering. For this reason, meeting the needs requires activity, people also cooperate and at the same time give guidance. As guidance, the need is personal quality. The key point (very critical) in understanding the place of needs in the state of mind is the problem of satisfying them.

Beyond all the science, wisdom and common sense, every person can realize that the centre of his life is the satisfaction of many needs. The person himself is a system of efforts to meet certain needs. Meeting the needs is not unhindered. On the one hand, there are laws, norms, rules of culture, and on the other, opportunities for people and, as a rule, societies where there is no justice. The third and delicate moment is when **the meeting of needs is experienced as pleasure.** The attitude of cultures, institutions, and people themselves to the consumption of pleasure has been different and still is. Everyone has the right to choose and the right to decide whether the experience of pleasure gives meaning to life or "Does life make sense if there is no pleasure? ". This factor - meeting needs gives value and meaning to life, and if so **Viktor Frankl says "we must say that dissatisfaction, failing in life, rewardless efforts make a person noogenically and existentially neurotic/traumatic."** Unlike animals, human beings are the most developed needy creature. This is because people inherit certain needs and at the same time acquire new needs and new aspirations. In this sense, the attempt to portray the human need system is often unsuccessful. There is a typology that takes into account the fact that humans are both biological and cultural-historical individuals/beings and gives a very clear idea of the ordering of needs.

There are three types of need:
1. **Biological** - vital/physiological/primary - these are needs that protect a person's life as an

organism. They are the most essential. They are not inferior. People are aware of them. In general, and especially in primary needs, their dissatisfaction makes life difficult.

2. **Social** - these needs express the life status of humans which is different from those of the animals. Needs from another person - the most social need - work - creating and maintaining social relationships more broadly. The lack of this need (extreme form) - alienation, loneliness among others. Relationship with others builds the personality, without other people there is no personality.

3. **Spiritual Needs** - the highest human needs and encompass such territories of the spirit as love, creativity, development/growth, belonging to a mission.

The role that needs play in the organization of mental life and the choice of behaviour under the flag of individual characteristics - each person makes his or her own composition of needs and arranges them in importance. Abraham Maslow did such a generalization by developing a rather original view of both the needs and their dependence on one another.

Pyramid of Needs:
1. Physiological needs
2. Safety and security needs
3. Needs of belonging and love
4. The need for recognition, respect, meaningful status
5. Self-actualization needs

The first 4 are called "deficiency needs" (needs for something). In its capacity as a motive after its satisfaction, the tension drops, goes to 0, while at the 5th (need for self-actualization) the satisfaction does not minimize the motivation, but increases it. Abraham Maslow thinks secretly that the lower a need is, the more important it is, and the less impossible it is to satisfy the next need. If the first 4 are not satisfied one cannot self-actualize. "The unsatisfied needs have to treat the satisfaction" Self-actualization is radically different from the other four. It is a movement to the talent.

Emotions and feelings.

Aristotle writes that there are **3 types of processes:**
1. Reason/mind;
2. Feeling;
3. Will/will-power.

We say:
1. Mental/intellectual;
2. Emotional;
3. Willings/volitional/strong-willed.

When we want to explain the nature of these processes, it is most reasonable to say "What do they give us?" Let's choose a popular life case. When a person confronts an object, a face, an idea, an object, **two questions arise:**
1. What is it?

2. Why is that so?

The answer to these questions is given by the mind/the reason, intelligence, cognitive processes. Ordinary consciousness identifies consciousness mainly with reason.

What does this matter to me personally?

Through reason, consciousness tells us what things are, but through other processes, it tells us what they mean to us, how valuable they are, how much we need them, how much we love or hate them, how happy or unhappy they make us. Consciousness is capable of revealing us the subjective/personal meaning of phenomena and events through processes called emotions and feelings or affective processes. These processes are the most intimate structure of consciousness and the unconscious.

Emotions and feelings - they are not cognitive processes, they are not feelings, they are not thoughts, neither fantasies nor representations. They are processes and states, experiences that unfold as pleasure and displeasure, as direct and indirect and multiple derivatives. They are states similar to themselves. These processes are reflected in what we call bias/partiality. Every individual consciousness is psychologically biased. The genesis of emotions and feelings cannot be understood without the connection with needs. The earliest reaction is emotions. Emotions and feelings signal the state of life (continues or perishes). If the need is satisfied, then the pleasure for the organism follows if the need is not satisfied, then in some circumstances, the organism perishes.

2 notions/terms:

1. Emotions
2. Feelings

Emotions mark the primary reactions, the appearance of pleasure or displeasure.

The term "feelings" refers to emotional experiences valid only for the person who has reached a state of personality. They are related to a typical human need. They may possess a person for a whole life. They have many properties that explain their nature better.

Main functions of the feelings:

1. **Assessment function** - through feelings one evaluates objects as significant or insignificant, as necessary or not, as positive or negative. Emotional evaluation is subjective. Not only the value of the object but also the peculiarities of the personality play a

part in its formation. The main thing is - "What satisfies the object?"

2. **Incentive function** - there is a motivational focus. Emotions and feelings often function as motives.

3. **Regulatory function** - we carry memory traces of emotional experiences. We have an emotional experience that strongly regulates what we need to do.

4. **Disorganizing function** - accompany each process. In many cases, emotions come in disharmony with mind/reason. Reason dictates one pattern of behaviour, feelings dictate another. Is it true that feelings can displace the mind, make the behaviour illogical/antisocial or vice versa - do people rationalize the feelings? And on this basis, in a very rough way, the harms and benefits of emotions are considered.

5. **Activation function** - special engine and activity accelerator. The mind gives a

solid foundation and the feelings give wings.

Emotions and feelings have an integrative function - they accompany all human experiences and can manifest ambivalently (both pleasure and dissatisfaction are experienced). Emotions and feelings are another second language of consciousness consisting of 2 words - pleasure/displeasure, pleasant/unpleasant, but these words are enough for the psyche to speak in all languages.

Final Words

Thanks to all the readers who were interested in this book. In it, I tried to make a concise and enjoyable synthesis of some of the most influential psychodynamic theories in psychology. I hope that each of you is happy with the reading and has acquired new knowledge that will serve you both in work and in life in general. Psychodynamic theories are one of the most complexes in psychology, and this brief synthesis neither exhausts this vast matter nor provides the necessary knowledge, but I hope it was a wonderful, interesting and enjoyable read. Best regards, Valentin Boyadzhiev!

www.ingramcontent.com/pod-product-compliance
Lightning Source LLC
Chambersburg PA
CBHW031227250726
48655CB00005B/1844